THE SPIRIT / THAT KISS

Works by David Annwn

Poetry

Shadings
Foster the Ghost
King Saturn's Book
The Other
Definitive
Primavera Violin
Is
Ffin
Flare Head Live at Leeds

Prose

Inhabited Voices: Myth and History in the Poetry of
Geoffrey Hill, Seamus Heaney and George Mackay Brown
Lines of Force: Presence, Spacing, Sign; the Art of Peterjon Skelt

Collections

ed. Catgut and Blossom: Jonathan Williams in England
ed. A Different Can of Words: Warrington Writers

Interview

ed. Peterjon Skelt, Prospect into Breath : Interviews with
North and South Writers

the spirit / that kiss

NEW AND SELECTED POEMS

1973-1993

David Annwn

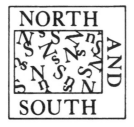

Twickenham and Wakefield

Cover photograph of Pt. Scheemaker's statue for Sir Michael Warton's memorial, Beverley Minster, by David Annwn; photograph of the author by Lesley Newland; book designed by Peterjon Skelt.

Published in May 1993 by North and South at
23 Egerton Road, Twickenham, Middlesex TW2 7SL and at
77 Lincoln Street, Wakefield, West Yorkshire WF2 0ED

Acknowledgements

The author wishes to thank the publishers of the following books in which some of the poems in this selection were first collected: *Shadings* (West Yorkshire Press, 1986); *Foster the Ghost* (Bran's Head, 1984); *King Saturn's Book* (North and South, 1987); *The Other* (Smith/Doorstop, 1988); *Definitive* (IS, 1989); *Primavera Violin* (IS, 1990); *Louis Zukofsky, Or Whoever Someone Else Thought He Was* (North and South, 1988); *Affirming Flame* (CPF, 1989).

The Spirit / That Kiss is published in a trade edition and in a signed edition of 10 copies lettered

S   P   I   R   I   T   K   I   S   S

ISBN 1 870314 22 0 Trade edition
ISBN 1 870314 23 9 Signed edition

British Library Cataloguing in Publication Data

A catalogue record for this book is available from the British Library.

CONTENTS

INTRODUCTION

It would be hard to state the central 'idea' of David Annwn's poetry without doing violence to it. It is too subtle, too lived through (experienced and composed), to be reduced to any abstraction.

The poems in *The Spirit/That Kiss* move between extremes of asking "How do I compose that day" and "millenia/ sun endlessly takes/aerial shots... Tre'r Ceiri re-assembled/ in the studio of light"; between the poet shaping a pattern by which he can understand his experience, and submitting to the larger pattern of nature and the cosmos. It is a poetry that negotiates between the human and the nonhuman. Its concerns are deeply human and humane — empathy is among its chief qualities, empathy with women's experience in particular — but it opens on the non-human universe, which gives a different measure to human concerns. A particularly striking poem is about two people arrested by a night migration of snails:

This stopped your argument,
your heated voice
going and coming on the mist;
this stopped the bringing out
and parading of a battered love.
This even frailer flesh
stopped us soon enough,
and the heart's contention
in mid-step

Generally, the poems do not stop the heart's contention — on the contrary, the poet wrestles with his and other people's difficult emotions — but they do set the human in the context of larger movements and rhythms.

What is evident from the beginning is the poet's feel for words and the music of words. Like his father in 'The Quarry', and like Geoffrey Hill in *Mercian Hymns,* and Seamus Heaney, he raids "the earth's dark hoard". His strong historical sense 'sounds' the history buried in words. In this respect, he is a poet drawing on a strong tradition of the British Isles —an old tradition which, from Eliot to Heaney to Hill, has been renewed in the 20th century. From the start of this book, the poet has absorbed his influences. He treasures words, he names and savours empowering his individual imagination. Nor is he identifiable in terms of this tradition alone.

Jazz is important to him, and his verbal music is correspondingly various, ranging from the uncomfortably edgy to passages of lyrical clarity. One thing it is not is facile. This is true both of the matter and the manner of the poetry, which combines a sense of national and family history with a strongly-felt engagement with contemporary issues. Indeed, it is a poetry for difficult times, written out of awareness of the conditions threatening all that poetry stands for. This is felt poetry, and poetry sounded in syllable and phrase and passage; but is also a poetry of the intelligence, exploratory in its thinking, testing the limits of what can be thought and said. For this reason, too, it eschews facility.

Jeremy Hooker
January 1993

For Lesley

HARDY

Never let the tear drop
From the tight prune face.
The wit is coupled up inside a broken chest
And old moons have grown tepid
Inside the watch-case eyes.
The faint moustache sunned
By autumns of long shepherding:
The magician's hands are magnificently scarred,
The stars blaze, barbs in the bleeding hide of sky,
Our herded cruelties belie compassion.
What is it that never lets me forget
When the ideal poet walks on stage,
    A boy who soiled his pants
    And shuddered at his father's mean irritation,
    Dark, angel-losing nights,
    And old men sadly congregate
    Above the railway station.

THIS ISLE WAS BRITAIN IN TIMES PAST

divers maskers enter
and sea-green herbs guard the burthen
All have a lovely parallel
the sun's babes, carantos, moriscos
And le grand Galliard, let fall a bright circle
As henge-stone they watch, subtle in day's curdled gold
faces solemnly gay, as the old sun pants his last dance out
    and outside the peasants die

mirrors have followed me round,
all day to find themselves in me,
finding all that the blind do, in houses massed with
lantern light,
 Bless me Anno Domine - to make this line vanish
Wind blows chaff; devour it.
 – Rain, rain falling on snow
   chiaro cristallo, chiaro, cristallo

TRE'R CEIRI

How do I compose that day —
spick slate, quarried flanks,
a jutting isle of mourners
where all who land turn black?
No scratchy lines
of foreign oarsman or cliff-leaner
humped in mist
reflect back to wind's abrasions.
Just rock, a tousled gull, the fall.

Jet declivities,
lesions, screes— no map
can quite help the eyes to the West
over the sunken keep of Vortigern.

Village boys leave their charcoal rings
in hut-walls now bare
to the scurry of breezes' steady dirges.

II

This peak is a grinder
for stones and fossil-fish.
The giant's silent eyrie
gazing, one-eyed, to ruins
where brogues faltered, then took the air.
'Adventus Scotorum'... gravities
sensed in that tall hive at Aberffraw,
dignitaries' combed minds,
crests, exchequers, varnished board-games
alive with coloured pegs.

Miles of terns and foreshore,
lines of nets strung out to sea
gathering and dangling
brown swathes of kelp.

III

Come glaze that tribal sneer
of cracked rock,

soften walls of farmer's speech.
Porth Dinllaen,
Llŷn of Leinstermen,
whisperings of those who weigh land
or dreamt of isles,
pitched like upturned coracles,
marigold faces of saints
between cloisonné leaves
stare beatas at the prowling beasts.

The sea became a whole still surface
for their blunt immramma.
Hammerhead prows
stubbing sandy groins
to the bodhran's mad batter.

IV

Did I seek to get these edges out of me
on this striated ground?
Uses of the heart,
'Wherein the lightsom leuin shroudes
so cleaves thy soule a sunder.'

One can probe too deeply and for too long.
I dropped through scuds of sheep
to the road.

Safe in bed it is easy to think
of how I wished to sleep
in among those rounded cairns —
a curl of bones like any other.
Up there
where the stars are dents in a shield
and
a whale has brushed the face
of the sea.

THE QUARRY

for Jeremy Hooker

I watched him raid
the earth's dark hoard,
drive his fingers through
the thick resistance
and drag it up to light,
glistening slime
around his wrists.
I could not hold it to myself
that these red-heavy globs
we cradled through the sand
could ever sire that mute array
of lip and spout
that stood so cleanly on our shelf.
But, half-angry and half-sad,
I followed in his prints
dragging plastic, sopping with the stuff.

II

My father sits,
elbows lodged in hips
and smoothes this face.
Watch an eddy spindling,
rippling slip.
Globe, newly red with birth.
He rims and wires it off
and stands away.
Does it crumble, melt?
The perfect touch of age,
pot laid in earth
millenia ago,
egg laved and rounded by the mind.
This moon of earth
to stand above my quarry.

LIGHT DOWN

In the snuck
of my mother's armpit,
freckled and downy, clung
a child who smiled
this way and that:
a limpet grin
nudging like a nose
wrinkling into her always skin.
Jealous of him,
I ground my gums,
snuggled urchin-like in ruffles,
nightdress folds and night perfumes,
rockpools so foamy I could not see his face.

I was her first
but always when the bulb gleamed off
those eyes peeped slyly out,
light's afterbirth
palely round her
dreaming, dormant curve.

Long afterwards, I realised
I was her dearest because I survived.
Not like this stranger,
dumb and lost precursor,
brother ghost
brought strangly limpid
from her womb.
He was the tremble on her lip,
her stumbling fingers
on the nappy's sunken frown.

He lay by me, dear God,
a gentle bruise on thought
she brushed like contours
round my head,
a wound she gently probed to hurt
to feel upon the hurt.

Those nights, sky a membrane,
I stared out over collapsing seas
where black ate black continually.
I gripped this tenseness to my heart
the spark of his brief surety,
to carry through to this strange life
a light gone down before me.

AFTERWORD

for Jan

Will we remember it ever?
Lost like an echo, a pulse,
That lonely, dark November
Our crossed lives crossed and once,
Unguardedly, we came away,
Sleep-walking in the evening
To pause above the city-light,
The half-built Georgian crescent,
Discussing shared, unhappy loves
And why we walked through rainworn stone
To stand awhile or care at all,
The buildings massed, the railings shone
And why your hand was in my own
As bats came out small-hunting,
Quick flicks of life in pirouette
For shimmerings, I can't forget
Your hand, the dark, the lights, the stone,
Though we, past shocks, have both moved on
And lie tonight somewhere apart.

ARGUMENT

I hear your heel scrape,
and torch go down like a flare.
Silver scribbles veer across the tarmac,
a thousand horns draw in against the light
as cars moan by,
and we are in the black again.
But I feel them,
soundless shells,
soft nubs of flesh toeing forward
for a hundred yards around.
We have stumbled blind into
a dusk migration
from the damp wood's mouth
and we cannot move.
I bend and see voluted horn,
snails in droves, webbed and chipped,
pouring on the road and walls,
violet adults and the young
like a shimmy of snot
with tiny organs gleaming through.
This stopped your argument,
your heated voice
going and coming on the mist;
this stopped the bringing out
and parading of a battered love.
This even frailer flesh
stopped us soon enough,
and the heart's contention
in mid-step;
here, where I cannot
come back to you
except by little deaths.

FOSTER THE GHOST

Here, down rotting panels,
A steadying hand
Brings up a stir,
Glistening orange, larval backs,
Woodlice curling in families.
The dry retch
In a trespasser's throat
Thickens almost pleasantly.

Gleaming coffin finished in black:
The Morris; its leather upholstery
Holds alternative creaturely dreams.
A tiny ikoned prancing bull
Flickers over the dashboard's grain.
Headlamps' bars and massive bulbs
Throned in uteral chrome recessions,
Filament-wires, delicate gates
Wait for the rush
Of workaday light.

Hiding — a thrush
Of hill-line hedge,
His plucked look over quarry and marl
Stayed the shears an inch from my face.
Neighbours discover in cast-offs, old nests,
Up to my hair's undisciplined privet,
Pale frequenter of shadows, wet leaves,
Warmed with his breath
White portions of web.

Softly now, for Foster the Ghost
Is going his rounds by your basins of clay,
Coming to you, red sand on his fingers,
Smoothing his look, the look on your face.

SPIKE ISLAND
for Ian and Maggy

If name and credit allow

Speculation and dirt and gold
Assume, in time, particular ends:
Here its landscape,
Fiddler's Ferry,
Here its giant — its foundering shore.

Children, dogs in dirty water,
Ice cream vans and the snoring
Velocity of model speedboats.
I falter here on gravel-stone,
I too come, investing my stare.

Dry-dock area known as the first.
These arches from the 1840s
No mere bluffs for Hutchisons.
Tersely, plaque of slate informs:
'Birth of the Chemical Industries',
Green mud shelving to the course.

What passes for air in the estuary?

II

'Spike' from 'lean-tos' navvies built
Might locate their labour still:

Bedded, the spars of the rivermens' 'flats',
Holds full of slime, resistant to tides,

Standing, a rudder, massive and hinged
Could be a door to lurid horizons.

In sandy depressions hollowed by breeze
My brother-in-law plants laurel and ash.

Splayed leaves and twigs are tibia here,
Imploring against conglomerate towers

And critical fumes, the flimsiest stir
Seeming important, purposeful, frail.

Your exorcism with mud and stem,
Re-earthing the mind — significant fossil.

AMULET

Thaw-water beads on blackthorn tines,
Ice-pure drops at intervals,
Pendant, globing from the stem,
Reflecting in their whiteness —
Total mass — the surge of hedge
Suspended, gleaming, miniature,
Curled into a tiny swirl
Of darkened, jagged strands like hair.

A SHORT ETYMOLOGICAL STUDY OF THE
EARLY HISTORY OF OSSETT, WEST YORKSHIRE

To blond incursors —
                    "the roof of a hill"
Fortifiable — "keel of a ridge".
For thundering destriers,
                    shambling mire —
One more summary massacre.

Pages of Domesday offer a mirror,
Glinting and dazzling. For 17 years

Hardly anyone lived around here
Except the hare's high predators —

Talons bridling on the air.

The
Abnegation of shock
Still shocks

'Honour', 'triumph'
'Casualty'
Staid inside
Those words

Notions of blood —
A motherland
The pleasure fittings
All ripped out

(1983)

24

TIME PIECE

Heat fronds the verandah, flakes the peeling paint,
Night becomes another mode of drinking.
The joint is empty, almost grey. 'And then there's us,'
He fills himself another glass and gazes at the watch
The mud-flats are starred by its gleam on the blind.
He'd been a long distance, and somewhere behind
The place he'd always meant to be.
But Joseph, ah hell, even winners get careless.
The coarse, heavy envelope had thumped onto his desk,
(Sounds like slack pulled from a sail)
Back in stiff September — the year before last —
September in Maine — so green and clear and brown:
Unailingly fresh — though that fresh thought is helpless now.
The flash of a paper-knife — the flash of a time-piece's
Gilt, initialled case: R.S. inscribed to Dear G.B.,
Cushioned in a soft-worn pouch of velvet.
The cutting and the mother's note enough to fledge his interest:
A long sweep of the Mississipp, a distant line of suspects,
A story in long-hand he somehow remembered,
Made dingier in the interim, Time's thumb smudging newsprint.
'Dear Mr Joseph Pearce — My Daughter' and her face
Shone thin and bleakly beautiful up from the artist's sketch.
Even he could see a grace, a keen-ness in those features,
A starve-acre rose on the trellis of her family,
Straggling up from dirt into bourgeois repartee
Or what's seeded of gentility that far into the rural West.
'Rural' — Why bless us sir — that's New Hampshire
Steaming in the gloaming,
Or views of Hardwick cusped in snow.
The River of America — where Europe meets the Jungle
In the Desart of its mind. In the sweat
The rank rind of slapping water
Is dead, dark, clay redness where it fingertips and licks the shore.
That first night on the steamer, a great sense of promise
Rose above the thrashing wake — the heads of the waiters,
Those rare honest blacks, (the coolies, as he thought of them)
Of raw Savannah's latitude, bred them for that service.
                    'The latitude of judges
Is much to be mistrusted', he proffered as he stared
Into warm, untenanted mist. Girls strolling on the aft-deck
Blurring with her features.

— Even her shadow was shadowy with white
Lucent as magnolia —no that's crass, he determined
A trace finickity down to his ox-bloods.
The mother's co-ordinates seemed intelligent,
At the outset of this excursion —come, hardly that:
                    The Witnesses, the Suspects,
Their Alibis, their Whereabouts and the precise nature
Of her blunt, staggered death, shot twice through the fore-head
And ditched in a sluice or, at least, this is what THE TIMES DEMOCRAT
Leader said, if he could believe what was left of it,
The paper reverting to pulp in his sweat.
A lizard on the deck! Grey and red and mottled like a gecko.
Time was that Grace's cull was on everybody's lips:
Coarse coalflatmen in the moral sties of Cairo and Orleans,
Madrid gin-palaces. Mud clerks in shape-shift steamer-berths.
The ghosts of keelboats and barges float past.
A phantom La Salle reflects in the green
As Joseph looks out from light in his berth —
          the moon's reflections over the surface
               wobble and vanish
                    into insouciance.

Looms,
          The dead tree, sycamore's snag
               Crooked,
                    Through sleep protruding, rotten
                         One-sided, indistinct...
'Labboard lead, there! Stabboard lead!'
'Quarter-less' is cried from the men on the hurricane-deck
into his dreams.
He wakes up over and over,
Finds he hasn't woken,
In a bedded hulk, in a windowed wreck.

The dense summer continues next day.
'A real Hum-Dinger.' The press remark.
                    '...that murky waste water'
Marryat once compared to a sewer
Annually empties four million tons
Farm-yard, pig-run, wood-slide mud
into the Gulf of Mexico.

'Well, fancy that, suh, just fancy that,'
Is always caving in its banks
Moving astray, sideways, thirty miles at a jump
Delving its arteries deep into farms —
                    the cabinned paupers' unreal estates.

                    Blind reefs shaved by the hull
For weeks the island foliage drags at the stern.
The chutes rising above Madrid — swinging with virulent grape-vines,
The forest thickness opens its depth
and the cliffs — flowering trailers, tender willow
Thickets giving out to cane. Scows and flats at Baton Rouge.
Tick-tack-tick — he'd wound it up to run awhile,
(It started as it never stopped)
When he'd first gained it and didn't think to let it down,
Her love's medallion coined by him: Robert Sullivan,
Sully to his friends — spoked around him, round a hub,
Principal suspect, died in gaol,
'Unspecified causes', read the copied letter-head,
Monogrammed Pen. certificate:
An eagle starred in flight, is that the state crest?
Sully had cause to be desperate;
                    he hadn't done it
Thought Pearce echoing the mother's indignant assay.
Since when did motive have a say in it
inside the old ballads?
The ancient muscular, thrusting prerogative:
Of mortal's innermost instinct,
Down by the banks of the Ohio
The Tay, the Tyne, blanched heroines are murdered
Only for their pert, destructible innocence,
The perfume of their silk-glozed blooms,
                    Crinolined Magnolia,
Rawness wafts to sense again, against his better side.
'Oh God, how long this sailing seems to take!'
His face in the mirror is scarlet, he sweats unkempt through his moustache,
The armpits of his shirts are deltas now of blackness,
Black as every sleep
                    — the thump of engines at his spine
The bells, the bells, the rapids
                    — at death's black, jutting barge
                    'Stabboard...Stabb-'
                    Shudders, cries.

'The State of the Union — Cause for Concern,'
Unstintingly sick of reading it,
The blocked and unblocked capitals
Etched onto his every thought.
The other readable matter aboard:
Stacked, ironic religious tracts
                        'Save your Souls!'
The cheap, gravure images: Christ whipped
By miserable, licentious, carpet-bag fools.
                Yankee go home, even here,
                        — on the border's moveable glisten.
'Down by the banks of the O-hi-o'.
                Young Schliemann had called it
Pearce's Pecadillo when he sent the money back
To Widow Blonchbonnier grieving for her daughter,
'I don't want your roll of dollars ma'am,
No, it's not that it's Confederate's...
                        I simply don't reckwyah it,'
A tipped hat, the reverent nod
To match Beauregard's — the uniform glove on the shrouded drum,
Revealing Northern courtesy for the recently-bereaved,
Forgotten by her own state kin — bereft. At loggerheads,
Sometimes he day-dreamt he'd never left his office.

The jungle, the cabins, the passed plantations
Are clouds in a sunset reflection,
Inked gaudily into an illustration
On a discarded cigar-packet,
Floating and slewing swiftly downstream.
Some slave might fish it out and covet.

The War was so mismanaged,
Lincoln and his cronies' short-sighted
Humanitarian sympathies.
Pearce cared no more than a match-stick for
The destinies of warring tribes.
Freedom, let them have it, as though it
was pre-ordained, that poor and rich didn't exist,
As though the feudal hypocrisies
Weren't well-embedded, into the matrix.
Now take the English,
They knew how to buttress a caste
With ethics and order and education.

So much he had learned in Britain
Where he had wintered away the war,
Taking an interest in that little case
Of frail Lord Chanctonbury's mistress.
The agency judged it apt, and pecunious.

The women had liked his foreign air
Of 'mystery, mystery, Mr Pearce,'
And he liked theirs.
Even young Indian 'widows',
Had helped him pass a year or three,
Rather 'suttee' than Gettysburg.

The scow takes him ashore,
His land-legs stumbling under him,
Happy to be off the river.

The hickory-crosses on share-croppers' graves,
A mass-grave of the shot and decapitated poor,
Soil the colour of shrivelling corn-pone,
The cracked echo of an axe-cut in sycamore,
Primes him, prepares,
(Did he dream all this?)
His skin is painted — the mirror,
Louis Quatorzed with scrolled mouldings,
Lays bare his livid,
Sun-crimsoned stare
Back at the other behind his eyes.
Under the eaves of 'Le Monseigneur,'
Evening ensconces, bats twitter, the whirling zones
of beetles unsheathing their droning, sudden focus of flight
And sudden, unruly splay like a horror
Caught in the curtains — small folk, torn limbs.
The crickets chirr
                — murder, murder, murder

The Blonchbonnier place all boarded-up
Together with others, two, three, four,
Spacious porches — true — but cheap-jack as well, and tarnished
And splintered with age. If someone had accosted,
Waylaid him brusquely and asked him to opine
What happened here, he would have said bad harvest,
A plague of weevils, lack of trade, lynchings — he faltered

Deep in his other life's prejudice yet.
But not as much as the passers-by
Still 'nigger this' and 'nigger that,'
Still he assumed the prospect of distance.

The pistol will lie in its Parisien case,
Morocco-bound ornate precision,
Its turned bone-boxes for patches - the rammer,
All sleeved in velvet;
Brushes, shells,
Assorted spare nipples and oil in its bottle,
Unctuous, awaiting emollient,
The slippery skin of lubrication,
Never to be used.

No-one knows her.
Even before he asks the questions, they answer
Look down at their chaw-filled sputum on the ground,
Top their drinks with gazes like a razor's.
Sully, no-one knows, nor the estranged mother,
No-one knows or knew or cares
To remember, has even a mind to either
Be made newly aware or recall the case.
The engaging law-officer in his quiet office
Flutters back through his files
                              – 'there's more to this
Than meets the eyes,' and *his* eyes flicker
At absence trying to re-suffer a mote that was there
Yesterday.
                Pearce's heart went out to his orderly,
Exotic neatness, his sensing out of decencies
Even in those who killed, driven on by the forced liquor
Of passion, deprivation, guilt.
                              The state's discretion
Was his, his finger on a file and turning from the wall
'No, it's not this one — this was Chubb's Creek, '67
And all those hotheads in the woods from the war,
And Lawrence was her name...'
                              'But surely —'
'But surely not,'
                And there it was again,
The note in the voice like a last restraining latch
On the door or a rifle's safety-catch

                                    between them, between
The twisting rays of their mute appraisal.
'Look friend,
                    folks round here,'
                                    his tab-touching finger
Cocked his lapel — a history of unsolved murders
Gliding by in his impassive stare.
                            'I'm from downriver a-ways, anyway,
                            Vicksburg —
                                    never really knew her...'
And had he really uttered her name,
Then as he stood in the office door,
As some unfriendly epitaph,
part-slurred,
Or had he mis-heard?

'This is a fair, industrious backwater and the folk,
Though often in oppressive straits, civil and generally speak
With friendliness. Though I say this with some hesitation
I'm forced to admit the over-riding impression
Of dirt, warm dirt wakened to threat of all kinds,
Though fully aware of how superstition
Mists my clichéd tone to you, it is different being here
Dreading Fall and Winter.'
Schliemann had to take the strain
                            and petty litigation
Now he was dogged and swamped
                            by obstruction.

The townspeople brooked his every approach
With nice indulgence — 'Le Nord', 'The gentle',
Some thought him English, his diction an example.
Even the sundry down-and-outs he chose to coach and steep
In memory with memory-steeping alcohol
Suffered his questions with wrapt largesse.
From Lethe, on the stream of their forgetfulness
He logged them — every landfall — every camp-fire tarradiddle
Be it e'er awry to their Helicon's bellicose mount
And founting fantasy, to each tale's tallest source:
Whupping 'bars' or sumptin' or Sumner
Or Finns or Irishmen
                            ...'or Sully,' he whispered
'Say Mister, you aren't from round about here
                                    are yew?' Snares
Begin to mouthe like watchful poachers.

The grain-merchant's son was her first-betrothed,
Pre-Sully's intervention. Had there been a family pressure?
Paul Rahilly farmed hogs, his father's adventures
Had finally over-shot his sights and sloggered into debt.
Pearce waited on mud rucked with dynasties of trotters.
It felt as wooden as a stage, this shifting, stinking ground had set,
Sled-hard. 'I felt you might have something...' the son limped
As he led him in '...to say?' 'That's my privilege,
For you to guess and me to stay: silent, I mean.
D'you get much pay in your kind of prefe - shun?'
Eyes watched him back way on through the wood

This is his revolver-case going into the river
To lie in its newer case of slime. A French box
With French hinges. This is the swimming-pool stirred
By heydaying black boys whitened from field-work.
This was one they shot. This is one they sternly-admonished.
Dust settles. Gauzes of mayfly-wings, tiny, freckled
Love-dances noticed by no-one over the narrowing iris
Dragged like the ball and chain of the eye.

Dead blossom flounders and blows.
                              The sincere
Hope to get something done gets nowhere.
The sheriff spends his days hoisting carts out of mud,
My money all but dwindles out, Jonathan —
Schliemann, for God's sake, this isn't such a mystery — her killer..
I spend my days tramping and questioning mule-skinner kin.
I shall spend October in Texas —
                  Vista on vista of inglorious prospects —
She was a shy girl on the surface,
La Belle — all right, demure — un peu, slight
Hesitancy like a lace commotion, bad nerves in the picture
Too. But, judging from character, Rahilly
Is no guiltier than Sully.
What quality was it led through this silence to its prey?
And closed the silence after?
I open the clasps on her watch, no image and no miniature music
As sweet as the steel that enters me then.

'The servants,'
              Through sleep, prompting Schliemann,
              have already been questioned.

32

So much is clear from THE DEMOCRAT's version.
I waited a day under clapboard and shingles
Rain cross-braiding its ambiguous streamers
Over the shelves of forested spurs,
The margins westwards gathered like muscles
Gorged with fat. The river's flat glisten is lost at my back,
The blacks are lost and gone right back to their scattered demesnes.
Who bears them malice? Which shrub holds densest colonies
Of grubs ready to shrive the parent-plant of health and hale-ness?
Which rumble of their past, of opening doors and holding hats
Makes them bolt and start fast from my furretting whisper?
They're flown in bents and thistles – shafts gone straight under corn.
The sun throws fitfully – feeding its incinerators.
They're gone seeking decency, honour, and I weep for their fear
And future conclusions.

This is the furthest east the senoritas spread.
I took one to me. West. Wordless. Stunned easy.
So different from *her* beauty, it was admissable
At dusk. A cleft honed into myself. Do not repeat this,
her hand smarting velvet, her throat. Let it be
A footnote in some stale inventory of careless
Lives. My face is the dead soil burnt for trees.
I am writing with the utmost respect for your conscience.

Revenant, I come back on myself at strange intervals
Of odd recognition. I crossed here three months
Ago. I asked at those tents.
So the ants bring back fragments, traversing the heads
Of their comrades, climbing old gulfs with bits of cut leaf
A sweet but rancorous scent in their mouths,
So the mansions of dreams are numerous,
So snake devours its vaporous tail.

The snow is gone before I wished it
However I have deferred the admission
Down-at-heel, obsessed, eating what I can
Schliemann. Jonathan.
I am as lost as that which I seek.
The watch-chain wears my waist-coat pocket thin.
My worldly possessions are pawned or abandoned.
Rest less and less
Pour whisky more.

Health suffers. My head's adrift with incoming summer,
The vast collusion of scent, stink, fragrance
Wilder than any parfumerie. A brothel-jakes
Of rankness. There I've said it, spin out from me
Seethe as in the glimmering,
                              evening. There, a calm is
Shame as settled, quiescent, as a jetty, an old harbour
In a childhood painting. I'm shamed I wrote and thought
Those things. How is Milsome Street, the Fulbright bar?
Your mother? How do you eke your stipendiary
Over lank months? Do you still see the Collins girl?
I shot but one human,
                        and that in perilled frame of mind
In Chicago. Miss Temple. Does she speak of me?
Does Rafe Stickney run for Congress?
My stars are against the consummation.
                                          From the start
Of this business. I've slept in places you wouldn't
Curse a scurrilous wharf-dog to. I've come to an urgent end.
I remain your obt. servant. Jos. Pearce. 1872.

She is the sky, the oleander bloom, the jacinth,
She is the river-pulse circling the strokes,
She is the wound, green spring of ailanthus,
The seeping 'v' envigor'd by the roots,
She is the flared leaves on the stable puddle,
She lives with her father - the spreader of rumour,
Estranger of secrets and multitudes,
She mulches, she broods on long-encrusted lies,
Long-dead. She worries her head about what's happened,
What astonishes. What she's lain down to,
The crew of her imagination open their legs
Aghast again, one retina listening to the watch,
Her eye-lashes flick their filigree with
Its ticking. Come back, come back, it says
Visit us in the far-off land of breath,
Break us to that rhythm. Prompter echo.
Salve the space you lead us through,
Where silence brims, diminishes,

One shot, two,

Geese rise up from the girding woods.

34

Three sections from *King Saturn's Book*

1. REDBANK

In blood-starred wars our common weal...

As Cromwell watched them from the farm,
Roundheads set on meet estate
Mobbed the narrows, took the crest,
And cannoneers, their minds repelled
By every lignite hiss and thud,
Rooted men and planted them
Skyward legs in scurried ground —

Sand well-versed in martyrdom,
St Oswald's offered sanctuary,
Cherished stone and hand-smoothed font;
Some screeched like rats
And slapped into the Mersey.

2. NUDE

What I would see:
Pale body's extension
Of the poem's loneliness.

3.

Snow is barbarous in its falling,
It comes down stilly, it flurries
Against the pigeon's rest.
Prinked by sparrow's feet
Still it is unsettling, forming
Levels of its unrest.

There was not, nor ever is
Place to regard the eye,
Space to guard the light-opening.
Rooms where mothers and fathers sit
Frame their children's glint
With caring, arbouring fingers.

Snow is unwinding all over the land,
Estates and gardens and engines,
Injurious, cold, its song
Shivered in that chill regard:
O God, the aged,
Breathing in their sleet-blown house.

Radio playing, blurs all day,
Lovers next door think she's gone;
Where is this terrible winding,
Undoing endless patience,
Of heart's clear stem,
Where I have offended, or not

Undoing the grace-knot, the snow?

LOOK

From chained fields blocked by houses
Came the unwary, wary fox
Over and through the cold verandah —
Wine-smells lingering after dinner —
Rivuletted the lawn's full curve,
Came first to darkness,
Encountered the road
Just where the flower-shop shuddered with Fodens,
Scammels and Fords slurring past.
There sat down this tame toy dog,
Looking like a picture of a picture of himself,
Snuffing at the faces streaming by under glass,
Whirring before him — and one of them mine
Caught in mid-argument, tensely steering home
With you here beside me aware of my temper,
Not what it was for or my sudden swerving stop
At something coming clear of the life that lives beside us.

THE FIFTH

Tonight the house beseiged by concussions
Of rocket bursting and fiery hail
Will seem to suffer — an animal
Run to ground, grown close to me,
Quivering, seeking a kindred fear.

An apple-core littered on a plate—
The stains of leaf on paving outside,
The porch-lamps glow their brailles of light
Stonily onto the West Yorkshire evening.

My sister echoed my father. This morning
Their words return through years, make bright
Me lying in this bed alone:
'There's no such thing as grey that's light,

To say *dark grey* is meaningless.
Grey is grey, just that,' they'd aver;
I never believed them and don't today.
Somehow their words seem necessary,

Wrong and right all at once. (These painters
You know, they're all the same.)
The curtain's stationary waterfall,
The lightshade's gentler shade of grey,

Wardrobe darker still — the window-sill:
And whitest white fanning the curtain-gap
Like light on St Teresa's brow
To clothe her suffering in ecstasy.

But here there's me and only me, remembering
What my sister and my father joined to say
All at once. It is my coincidence,
The morning opening Guy Fawkes' day

To wonder at the shades of grey
Before such incandescence
Rips the night so far away
From our perception of it?

DEFFER INCIDENT

for Alison

Yellow-hammer gives a clue
As do the chiff-chaff's startled notes
Weaving a nest between the trees
To make us still.

Though all the rest is chaos:
The wood — the hill is blank and confusing,
The many types of vegetation,
Blurring offer no paths or answers.

I'm standing very close to you,
The way you gaze or purse your lips
Begins to come familiar.

— Keep still, keep very still.

OPENING — L.Z.

'Do you prefer your poetry to mine?'
— 'a kind of mathematics/but more sensual'

A train's cantata shrugs like breath—;

Of a Vermont sunset: 'Why should I praise it
I had nothing to do with it'—

The Zeebrugge disaster — P & O pickets
Rift the wind. The courts sequester bodies.

This is my face. This is my form
And the Passion of Matthew:

'break in grief, thou loving heart;'
"I heard him agonizing, I heard him inside"

Reticulations and out of them
Stems of the singing of voices,

Videlicet —
'The faithful poem is an act of conscience'

Shaken, open,

A rage instilled to
Tensile grace

A style of leaves

RIDER

The fifth
of the Apocalypse
Reins in
Stalls and rears in the charred index
of dollars and yen
His cracked macro-lenses
Take in
His gristle-breath listens
Blasted towers of the city
Beckon on, on.
Takes a light check
on his stocks
The flattened foundries
Myths of communities wither at his stare
Mind-on-a-gantry
Whirrs toward what vista?

The hearts of cot-deaths
ripped guts of Bluff Cove
some in Gucci saddlebags
Nicotine dribbles from glazed pores
Ozone blears, he sticks a tuft
Behind his lapel
It smells so sweet in dying
It's a fine day to scythe
He has come a long way
Yet never far enough.
The look in his face is oddly familiar
Yet not male. Human.
Not human.

ONLY A PHASE

For a full four months,
For the bus-driver taking my fare,
I am, of a sudden, the fat woman.
To my neighbours in the greengrocers
I am understandable, a naive tragedy
On legs: 'How long is it now dear?',
For my friends I am a chart
Of embarrassment: from morning sickness
To the breaking of unpredictable waters.
For my husband I am cosseted contraband
Calling forth an anxious schizophrenia:
'Let me carry that,' or 'I'll get it';
In the landscape of the bed
An uncomfortable hummock
He negotiates warily
As it sleeplessly turns and sags.
For other men — my colleagues —
I'm a state of body which never
Gets mentioned and eyes that never
Flicker below chin-line any more.
For my mother,
I'm the leadweight soon to grow a sinker
To plummet us close together again.
To old school-friends I'm literally a scream
In a hazy mirror — their hands touch me
Like toe-tips trying water.

And for you,
What am I for you?
You are the one suspended judgement
I lean upon,
A cave around its stalagmite.
I am your one element.
Mooning from me,
you'll split apart
This pod, this husk
Of memory;
No mercy
Just mortality,
Just one last echo
Lost in your eyes:
O Blood
Of My Blood.

Nine poems from *Definitive*

Out of stone
The maze
Emerges, of voices.
I must go seek
One I've known before again,
Mouth's hollow
Open to its orb,
Companionable void
That needs me too,
Who fosters who?
How long I wonder
Was the singerless echo
Waiting for me there?

My slate is always clean,
The rain makes sure of that.
My great-grandfather died
Under it cutting it
On a berg-swept hill in Wales,
The mountain for nine children,
So now these things,
And other things will never be the same:
The rain-coloured slate,
Slate-coloured rain.

HERE IT IS

Tailed and tilted,
Drifting in quiet
Down through the air,
Wonderfully light
And limber,
Its trim freight
Precisely-balanced,
Lifted on a falling breath,
Narrow-boned, its skimpy grace
Too slight, too slight, you say, perhaps,
Too featherweight to matter,
Settling gently inch by inch,
Alighting on your
Listening finger.

Miles with pink Mohican-cut,
His hand trembles, he looks away:
'Sorry David I haven't been able to get
This work done.' Hell, that's all right
Only, he finds it hard to put
Pen to paper, feelings flood, inhibit,
Draw the trembling hand back to the face.
Light is on your gentle, nervous smile,
Unbothersome boots stuck under the desk.
Your head ducks, doffs your shrill pink crest,
I understand its gorgeousness offsetting gray
On the winter trees. 'One more thing Miles,'
I say as he rises to seek out his place,
'Get it together, man,' I write on his pad.
He risks a grin of disbelief
At one ridiculous Hippy cliché
Almost twice his age.

I want the ordinary words
To yield
Nothing;
I want the words of their own accord
Especially the tired
Words that give their words
To several hundred different kinds
Of pent, forgotten tenderness
Left out in the corridor
All night,
I want their passed-over
Understated light.

Berio's beautiful ice-floe memorial,
A berg of sound with glitter
Of violin and shivering trumpet
For gulf of wife. I, fogged, glide on
Beside the leisure park in white
Slow, a cortège, stopping, stalling.
If I put out my voice
It would vanish at once —
The only remainder of words would be
A pattern of needles etched in a wave
Smeared across the screen.

SNAP

Janet Jeal of
The ambulance crew
(For nearly nine years)
Says it's a good service — the pay stinks
Morale has never been lower
People don't think of us
Like the Police or Fire Service
They don't think of how vital —
Janet Jeal hasn't time to eat
You grab hamburgers — you grab fish and chips
Fergie announces
Her new pregnancy
THE SUN is piqued they didn't spot it
The bookies clamour
20 to 1 it'll be a boy
Delivered privately in a private clinic
In Berkshire parkland, rushed to coincide
A new mansion rises for the happy couple
A nation waits with baited breath
For a child to join the landed classes
The stupidity of the English
Is insurmountable.

It must have been long
Ago, my father lifted me to
The fishers in the coracle

Brown salmon drove into the wall

Strip the sapling clean
Bend it to the frame
Tan the skin and waterproof

Sit down, it will hold you.

I like the sound
Of parapluies gris
It is a joy
To open the door
To see you again
As your face takes on
Its sweetest light
Like shade defines a surface.

I like the sound
Of gray umbrellas
Murmuring through rain
And young Bill Evans
Playing 'My Foolish Heart'
Testing the air
Forever.

TRIAD

"He has gone,"
Says my mother,
Meaning that her grandson,
Sprawled like a spent swimmer
On the settee,
Has gone out into the seas of sleep.
Somewhere his mind
Swoops over itself.

This afternoon
We climbed down into
The chasmed valley.
Rocks hacked from eternity
Arrived on time, ate our cries.
The trees had stopped
In gaunt diagonals.
The waterfall in drought
Had slipped below its steps of slate
To whisper like a ghost.

The clock ticks on and on.
Within the room I start to relive
How at fifteen I waited out boredom
And ran down scree on the side of Garn Fadrun,
Not thinking which leg to fling in front,
But blindly falling, forward, down,
Limbs hit up to the wheeling trees,
Lost in a meaning I did not make
I run, run, from start to finish —
A shuddering chain, a jagged cascade,
A torrent in spate of flesh-coloured stone,
A staircase of images all myself.

DRIVE

We are riding dark on an artery of dark,
Singing half-remembered choruses
Along the 401: Trenton, Belleville, Brighton,
All points West. Moths and brief insects
Are shedding their brittle incarnations
Against the glass of the speeding screen.

No-one remembers all of the words,
Each starts well with a burst of nostalgia —
Glenn Miller Drive goes flaring past.
'Let me call you sweetheart, I'm in love with you,'
'I'm gonna sit right down and write myself a letter,'
'Aint misbehavin', Savin' all my love...'
A serry of the Beatles Hits,
Lift as if it were yesterday
Lennon stepped forward in the glare of the Shea.

My mother is searching her mind's back roads,
For songs her father breathed her way,
Over her restless cradle:
'White folks are you listenin',
In the mornin', there'll be a christenin' —

The vastness of conifer
Stretches silent to the tundra.
One by one the phrases fade,
Glow for a moment,
Flicker and vanish as
Snowflakes on our tongues.

EARL 'FATHA' HINES

Out of the thickets of cold-water flats,
Cautered lives and indigenous racists,
Chords stung blue and cold by existence
Gold-slipper it into St Louis Boogie-Woogie.
He makes Fats Waller sound like Gershwin,
A little blues lament — a big production number,
Ragtime resounded in a Classical key,
Strutting out of Darktown to the Grand Terrace Shuffle
With nary a pratfall of dissonance, blunder
Or tinkling finger losing its way.
The lyric sweet grace of things how he plays them
Is a magic, a sigh settling down the spine,
The ease of walking a sunlit promenade
But he's the Brakeman of Thunder when
The thudding Pities call for it: The Song of the Volga
Boatmen is thumped out desperately keen,
The rhythm like rail-trucks slamming together
Till a mother's lost lullaby lost on the breeze
Spirals its stream on the doom-laden air.
And he always has time, one hand suspended —
For the child who dances without knowing why,
For the opulent, generous dreams of the poor
Stacked behind cracked panes of glass —
The manic daily Harlem cakewalk,
Stunned, lobotomized workers,
Lorca's blanched negroes dodging the traffic,
Stoked up on amphetamines,
That old frenetic tap-routine
Wearing the button-topped leather thin.
Our last and first Stravinsky of jazz,
His wandering arpeggios always returning
Through a gap in the wall to the gleam of New Orleans:
"Do you know what it means..?" his eloquent questions
Touch us like a tremor heard inside,
And there she appears — his Honeysuckle Rose,
Agelessly young, helplessly amiable,
Loving, Muse-like, delectable as ever
Beside the Mississippi running into Summer.

PERSEPHONE

Does she ever get used to it?
The anthracite throne,
The longing below for the fields above,
The piles of his dusty, work-stiff clothes?
And what of his silences,
Long and stygian in the hall without echo,
How does she pass the depths of her time?
Does she knit?
Play 'Throw and Fetch' with Cerberus?
Does she even develop a fondness for him:
Emperor Hades, Dis to his friends?
Does she learn to grow patience from hatred
And water in secret that bitterest bloom,
A grudging affection gloomy as nightshade
Rising from the ash that is her heart?

MIRANDA

In my dreams someone opens great caskets
To find a child's clothes smelling of the sea,
And someone opens cases in an echoing corridor,
(There is a crashing, banging)
To let out all the searching of the wind.

Someone is giving me words to say,
I am a valuable, a whorled brooch with Tritons
And aquamarine. I am a give-away
Keepsake. I look in the mirror — see my white face

With pinched narrow bones.
The day all the boys stopped to look at me
For the first time, I cried, not knowing
This stairway world of dense encounters.

I was posed in a tapestry of fierce caravels,
The coral of my spine
Was sleeved in crushed velvet.
I was the ikon you kept by your bed

For twelve long years. Look at me change:
Child, daughter, stranger through the swirling
Of your memory, grope back to feel my voice
As close by my side
King Naples sleeps wine-stupors off.

I am feared across the palatines,
High women bend their necks
Like peacocks to me,

This year I am fifteen.

FUTURE DAZE

'WHY HOLIDAY ABROAD TO GET YOUR SKIN CANCER'
Remember that make-shift poster's scrawl
Without a question-mark? He'd pulled it down,
That was the year the ozone had gone
And children stayed indoors. I'd known him
From school — we'd shared the odd Twix bar
And played his Walkman under the desk.
The first time I saw him in uniform
I'd known — something moved inside me,
A strange pattern: Regret, envy, admiration
And maybe something else.
We'd meet occasionally off-duty in a club
Or pumping the Pec Dec in the Precinct gym.
I can still see him — muscles glistening,
A gliding exertion — hand tearing words.
Then later, that Summer, the heat grew and grew,
We stared as through a greenhouse roof
At thin unnatural clouds. The politicians stewed
In obsolescent verbiage. The students threw
Riot after riot and the truth was unspeakable
For money owned the truth — everyone knew that:
The mill-edged maw was dumb.
And, as for my friend, he bought his all right,
He got it in the head in the famous March for Bread
Of 2022 — a righteous cause if any was,
Simmering wheatfields redly scorched,
Shades of the 1860s or even 1980s
When Thatcher ruled the roost. The picture showed him slewed
Across some loosened paving stones —one black boot
Wrenched to show his instep, delicate and nude,
A fallen Adonis, I found myself thinking,
Quoting old poems, God knows whose
Or cares any more. For suddenly I see
Vast vaults of books in libraries
Cruising to oblivion —all those serried
Dreams and private hopes we cling on to,
Our simian need to jabber on paper,
Drifting to nowhere, and no-one left to read
His brown blurred image staining my fingers,
The tear across my mind and the bricks showing through.

Seven poems from *Primavera Violin*

YOU PAINT THE VIOLINIST

I lean under your beam:
Head and shoulders emerging
Struggling — the theme — the player listens,
His whole body
Becoming the loll and 's' of a stem
Attentive, upstretched along his self —
'I don't know why I chose him
Or why Kerinthy for his story —'
Pause — moving around inside your mind
Prior to uttering. 'There's something, something...
Very human about a violin,'
And then, that quizzical uplift of brows:
'Don't you think so?' a curve of mind, heart
Wood, strings, your violinist soars in yellow.

1090 — nine hundred years ago
While pig-headed kings burned with feuds
'The country was utterly ruined
Unjust taxation and other misfortunes,'
After three Labatts the screen sits easy,
I read these six gold decals on the can.
It's not the Poll Tax or the cameras lined
On rails to focus another royal child
Through minds obsessed with luxury
And gain: it's not the gratification
Of the City and the men on the make of the moment,
It's not the raping of landscapes or waves,
It's the head of Blake's shepherd
Lifting sudden hope to the child in the cloud.

Our fake Strad hung around the house
Gathering dust for years. Its little prow
And coffin-swirls lay bare of strings
Mute, unplucked, f-shaped sound-holes.
Laid in the palm-flat it was all gloss
Warming to bosom-warmth. Easy to develop a taste
For just holding it like a backward child
Who never spoke or flew around the rooms.
The must of its interior was only thin dark.
Its intelligence was a slight continuous swoon,
Perhaps it was a pharoah's canoe bare of model mourners
Or a cradle for song borne out of rushes
In some marsh. It was a keepsake, though, be sure of that,
The music of its form almost outweighing silence.

The remembered stream was 'Balne'
Not 'beolne' creating henbane beck —
But a watering place, like German: 'born'.
I stand, its trill and churr
Glide by my feet as cars screech at the corner
And lights of the Prison waver on the field.
By day you see the detritus
Of plastic, street-signs choking its neck
And curve of crouched elder and hawthorn
Waiting to break into white, white
An upsurge of freshening
From tight green of the hidden root.
The estates tell you this is no-man's land for poets.
The beck plays its small pipes anyway.

AIR FROM ST JOHN'S

Moss in stone grooves
                in Names
Grass has overgrown all but faces
                of stone
A coverlet, no,
                and a few last
Letters sometimes left for light
To pick at, hardly recognize
Love's palimpsest
For she who went looking:
        Aged 2

        Brief flowers
        Treasures
        flowers planted

All turf has left of mason's craft
On some the grass leaves only stone
and one reads simply

        song in my

NADINE II

If I could start it all again
Would I eventually cover it
Like the marshes at Saltfleet,
Salt-bitten, fragrant and raw
With the yellow of rape gusting out
Of inland fields cut from view
Someone carrying the big blue oblong
Of a kite wearily home
Over the ridge; would my time with you
Re-create the land the sea loves,
Even one layer of it
Where larks at evening, eight
Rise straight through spirals
Of climbing song like mountain-peaks
That glitter high and won't stand still.

George, I thought I'd write you a letter:
May this be your year and the next and the next
Black, shale, green, light yellow, umber
What avenues a man might walk in distant cities
A violin inside his head? What's distance?
Or, at least, what is the avenue inside him
One outside has made — they meet, inter-glide
Become orient. Lightning plays about its surface;
Slate gaze. Hard facts. Your rivers have been
The Danube, the Thames — powerful cellos deep down,
Mine the Dane, the Ystwyth and Rheidol
One sluggish — the others sprightsome meandering twins
Now we are tributaries of the poisoned Calder.
Through murk may it raise primavera violins.

'ROUND' FOR TEOKRITI

Song within the poem
Opens, as a rivulet

To make a cup for thought
As one the Calydna ferryman

Sold to give as a gift
For a song: shepherd to goatherd.

More temperate with height,
Etna greens: fern and oak

As the song said. The cup's lip
Carved with ivy tendrils:

The scene of suitor-rivals
And fisherman — a cricket in a cage,

A little boy absorbed, lost to thought
The cup fresh-washed in wax,

Fragrant still with the wood and the thought
Which carved the cup and shaped

Its patterns, curved on absence
Scented. My uncle herded sheep

And sang. Four young men once in Wales
Met to mix their words for a river,

Steep lanes of ash
Their confluence — I've heard it said

You might as well sing — can't take your song
Away with you — though not your song or thought,

Give it for the gift of the cup
New-carved — goatherd to shepherd,

And let a spray gleam at the rim
For thinking's most neglected shape

In song these days. Sing as you will
I won't cut you short — I'll hear you out,

Your ravellings — though there is stress
And silence cuts, we have all day

To make a thought the shape of a cup

As a rivulet opens
Poem in song.

EVERY new
    every new
                splits only.
vine steel
vary blue spars   claw —
brace   brick

give back
every new very
you   evening
very —   roof-view
lit shards   —   sure moments building
now say it OUT // VEER

— Miles Dewey Davis III —

NEW YEAR

Orb
of baby's head
Streams quiet.

On the far side
Of glass
Loch sits black.

On the screen
Pluto's outermost moons
Explode in craters
Of white ice
Through dirty miles
Of ether and packed ice.

Under eye
Botticelli:
The Mystic Nativity
High dancers
Let fall their crowns.
Melancholy
Stillness within
Their joyful stride.

———

Salt moon:
That taste
We issue

From — 'as if the
Essence of origin.'
In their tombs,

Curved horn
And stone:
The long-necked birds

Free of feature,
Just the flight —
Past all.

Birds on their necklaces.

Sometimes we seem
A flex of air
In light,
That's all.

Moon-egg
Wind-mirror
Surface and centre
Clasped in one
Through zero night

LESLEY'S WINDOW

Eighteen glass panes set in three frames
Transparent oblong set in white plaster
Swathed in pale lace patterned with flowers
Of swirling lace. White light and sky through
Glass and lace; real leaves of the trees
Through patterned leaves, their green-ness paled
By the white of the lace — all this in a space
At the end of the house, level with my face
And eyes. My face is full of the light and
Swirl of trees through white, light's breeze
Brings all together, the thought of it
And these simultaneities,
Delicate incandescence.

TRE'R CEIRI: TWENTY YEARS

stone that
   clanks like
     metal

———

spring   : worts tinkle
summer : spores
autumn : orange grass-stain

———

take away
the rocks
you take away
the mountain

———

grey and mottled as
         a shark's back
stones rolled black
      beam through crock
      shark eyes

———

a stone skeleton
   scattered
disjecta membra
extract its thoughts
and give them names

———

all you will find
are empty circles
in circles
a camp-fire
cauldron of space

in rock-hollow
egg-shaped
pool
swallowing
the sky

—————

how rocks
        discord
discard like parted
           friends
and crowds
      peel, peel

—————

a river
of hills and mountains
unravelling at eyes —

runs away
high slipstreams

—————

these things:
a stem char-ringed
heather-root,
wind and sun-bleached
a star of wool.
filament
nerve of the orange grass

—————

the hawk
is a peak
compacted
running down its own
          dark flanks

the wind speaks
        silence.
earth makes this moan
            through crevices.

———

each tip of
fern's
a Tre'r Ceiri
a rusted, unscabbarded
dagger of bronze

———

millenia
sun endlessly takes
aerial shots:
each stone and rock
and shadow,
every direction and time
how slant light catches
brings,
every day, then out
— of memory
Tre'r Ceiri re-assembled
in the studio of light

IN DRAX

In the church at Drax
Under the power-station towers,
Wall paintings of the saints

A robin
To our side, rounded, its shape
A winged almond-eye,
Buffed.

My hand already
Can feel its life
As if it sheltered
Wing, eye, throat

In the church at Drax
Dreora Ac
Oak of the animals
Oak of the people,
Fragments of an abbey

In Drax
Willow Row
From the same place as Wealh
Means strangers

It is here the Angles decided
To stop their journey up the fens
Farmed next to Celts,
Voices over streams.

'We should be men...'
                    we should be women

Waggons and girls on waggons
Children light as lath
Winnowings in their hair

We should be men
            Not harriers

Give me a new sign of beginning

"What was the spirit that kiss was given in?" NC, 27/5/90

David Annwn was born 9th May 1953 in Cheshire of Anglo-Cymric parents. At Aberystwyth, Wales he met Robert Duncan, Ed Dorn, Gunnar Harding as well as being taught by Jeremy Hooker. He was part of the "Gallery Poets" Scheme and received a PhD in Modern Poetry in 1981.

In Yorkshire he co-founded N.A.W.E., and has given readings and led workshops at Lumb Bank and many other settings. A recent interview was published in *Prospect Into Breath* (1991). Vernon Scannell, choosing his work for *A Yorkshire Anthology* called him "a true original". He is great nephew of the Welsh Bard Ap Hefin — "Son of the Summer Solstice".

Contemporary Literature from North and South

Poetry

David Annwn, *King Saturn's Book*
David Annwn, *The Spirit / That Kiss: New and Selected Poems*
Richard Caddel, *Against Numerology*
Kelvin Corcoran, *The Next Wave*
Lee Harwood, *Rope Boy to the Rescue*
Geraldine Monk, *The Sway of Precious Demons: Selected Poems*
Eric Mottram, *Selected Poems*
Frances Presley, *The Sex of Art*
Catherine Walsh, *Short Stories*
Jonathan Williams, *Metafours for Mysophobes*

Prose

Bobbie Louise Hawkins, *The Sanguine Breast of Margaret*
Elaine Randell, *Gut Reaction*

Interviews

ed. Peterjon Skelt, *Prospect Into Breath*